A New Role for the Institution of Waqf

Hussein Elasrag

A New Role for the Institution of Waqf

Hussein Elasrag

The Messenger of Allah (peace be upon him) said: "When a man dies, his deeds come to an end except for three things: Sadaqah Jariyah (ceaseless charity); a knowledge which is beneficial, or a virtuous descendant who prays for him (for the deceased)."

This Book

Islamic social finance tools have been instrumental in the alleviation of poverty and socio-economic development for centuries. It was time that formal Islamic finance goes back to its core ideals, extending its impact over the entire landscape of economic development. The recent global drive towards a more equitable existence is acting as catalyst for the resurgence of formal Islamic social finance such as waqf. It is hoped that this could significantly contributes towards unified approach to global equality and achieve a 'better world'. There are novel approaches to more effective management and development of waqf institutions and the endowed assets. The general concept of waqf should be familiar to us as a predecessor of modern trusts and endowments. The waqf institutions can play important role for promoting global efforts to achieve our twin development goals i.e. ending extreme poverty and promoting shared prosperity in every country in a sustainable way.

Although some have argued that the practice of waqf may have existed well before the advent of the Islamic religion, Islam was in fact the first religion to develop a comprehensive legal framework that promotes, guides and fosters the development of the institution of endowments and charitable trusts. A donor endows a waqf with an asset and, in doing so, makes an irrevocable transfer of that asset, while also stipulating the intended charitable use of the funds it generates.

Waqf, as an important Islamic institution that underlies economic development, has been effectively utilized since the early Madinah period to inspire economic growth and expansion. The benefits it provided encompassed economic, commerce, education, health, social and spiritual dimensions.

Awqaf can be used not only to provide immediate necessities to the poor, but also to create or strengthen business support institutions that can lower the cost of doing business for the poor. Awqaf can also be used to support and build infrastructure institutions that can improve corporate governance and reduce the cost of doing business. For example, information bureaus, market regulatory bodies, the provision of accountancy services, and other such shared services for a group or for the entire society can be funded through waqf.

The latest statistics in United Nation's Global Issues report show that almost half the world's population or over 3 billion people live on less than US$2.50 a day; 640 million live without adequate shelter; 925 million people suffer from hunger; 400 million have no access to safe water; 270 million have no access to health services; 10.6 million died before they reached the age of 5 and 1 billion are illiterate. Therefore, the urgency in implementing funding instruments such as waqf that are aligned to the belief system of contributors and needy communities alike, has not been more pronounced than now.[1]

As one of the social finance tools, waqf has been instrumental in the alleviation of poverty and socio-economic development for over the

[1] https://www.inceif.org/2018/09/13/world-bank-inceif-isra-hold-roundtable-on-maximising-social-impact-through-waqf-solutions/

years. It has been adopted and applied even outside the Islamic world. –Its contribution to social development has been exemplary. For example, Waqf (endowment) has been utilized at the establishment of the Oxford University's Merton College in 1264. Throughout Islamic history, waqf was the main provider for many of the social services that today are financed by the state, including for education, healthcare, infrastructure development and maintenance as well as social welfare provisions for the poor and destitute. Waqf institutions have also supported a more equitable distribution of income and wealth as wealthy individuals and families released property into the service of the people for 'doing good'.

Although a significant number of waqf institutions exist globally, the success of these institutions relies on efficient governance, regulation, supervision mechanisms and effective management. Since most countries and regions do not have enabling waqf regulations or monitoring processes, the value and output of Awqaf assets are mostly on the decline. The potential, however, is enormous. Thus, this book focuses on the application of these concepts and some possible roles that waqf may play in the socio-economic development of the Muslim societies.

Contents

I. Introduction:

The institution of waqf, has played an instrumental role in addressing a range of socio-economic issues in the Muslim societies of the past. Many contemporary Islamic economists contend that the institution of waqf is still relevant to the socio-economic development of the Muslim societies, most of which face a multitude of problems. Social aspects of Islamic economics through waqf have been given little interest in Islamic economics literature, comparing to the Islamic finance and banking sector. The reason for this gap in the literature is mainly rooted in the challenges of collecting data and the measuring of Awqaf. The Waqf in many countries, and its Payment channels are mostly unreported and unclear, which is a clear obstacle for conducting an academic study. In this regard, there are several studies on understanding waqf and mostly, based on empirical studies such as surveys and interview analyses from some Islamic countries. But In many other countries, the studies on waqf are less than the other countries in spite of the people's high sensibility in this countries on waqf as an charity of all Muslims. The scarcity of studies on waqf may arise from the la

ck of data and the lack of transparency in the economic and political structure of the many Islamic countries. Awqaf can be used not only to provide immediate necessities to the poor, but also to create or strengthen business support institutions that can lower the cost of doing business for the poor. Awqaf can also be used to support and build infrastructure institutions that can improve corporate governance and reduce the cost of doing business. For example, information bureaus, market regulatory bodies, the provision of accountancy services, and other such shared services for a group or for the entire society can be funded through waqf. Thus, this paper focuses on the application of these concepts and some possible roles that waqf may play in the socio-economic development of the Muslim societies.

II. WAQF: Definition and Types

Philanthropy and benevolence occupy a central position in the Islamic scheme of poverty alleviation and redistributive justice.

Islamic social finance comprises instruments and institutional structures that are rooted in philanthropy. Their integration with for-profit risk-sharing instruments may provide some key success factors while addressing some critical challenges. The broad instrument of Islamic philanthropy is sadaqat. When made compulsory on well-to-do Muslims, sadaqat is called zakat. When sadaqat results in flows of benefits that are expected to be stable and permanent (such as through endowment of a physical property), it is called sadaqat jariyah or waqf. Contemporary Islamic economists emphasize that a philanthropy-based intervention inherent in the institutions of zakat and sadaqat could potentially take care of the basic needs of the extremely poor and the destitute and create a social safety net.

Awqaf have been used by Muslim philanthropists in the past and at present, in pursuit of religious satisfaction. Although it is a common assertion in the Islamic literature that waqf is a unique Islamic financial institution, there are parallels in other traditions as well. For examples, endowments and trusts in the Western world are like the institution of waqf. Admittedly, such developments in the West took place much later than the use of waqf in Islamic countries, and it is possible that trusts and endowments were an Islamic influence in the Western world.

Many Islamic scholars agree that waqf is a shariah compliant charity. They referred to general and specific evidence.

Allah - Exalted be He - in His revelation said about charity, including waqf "By no means shall you attain Al-Birr (piety, righteousness - here it means Allah's reward i.e. Paradise), unless you spend in Allah's cause (al-Imran:92).

Definition of Waqf:

Waqf is a form of charity for the sake of Allah. It is lawful because it aids in the sustainable development. It also seeks to empower the Muslim society. Waqf is a beautiful loan to Allah - Exalted - Who shall reward the endower granted it is done with pure intention.

Waqf, in the Arabic language, means to stop, contain, or preserve.

In Islamic terms, waqf refers to a religious endowment i.e. a voluntary and irrevocable dedication of one's wealth or a portion of it - in cash or kind (such as a house or a garden), and its disbursement for shariah compliant projects (such as mosques or religious schools...).

In other words, Waqf is a genuine Islamic formula which reflects that interaction between the values of faith and the values of development in Islam. These values distinguish the spirit of Islamic societies from that of other societies - that spirit which reflects the role of waqf in maintaining a society's identity and coping with its developmental requirements.

Linguistically speaking, Waqf means withholding or retaining, but on the terminological level, it means withholding an asset, which could be a house, an orchard or cash money or the like, so that it would become unsaleable and inalienable while directing its usufruct to a legal channel of spending.

An owner of a property, house, orchard or cash money or the like may dedicate any to a legal channel of spending on an ongoing basis. In this case, neither the waqif nor the nazir (administrator) of waqf are entitled to sell, offer as a grant or bequeath the asset being dedicated unless its usufruct becomes expired, in which case it can be disposed of provided that its proceeds should go to the same destination . In validating the legality of waqf, Jurisprudents (Faqihs or men of learning) relied on evidence from the Holy Qu'ran, the Sunnah, consensus and reasoning.

Waqf in the Holy Qu'ran

Due to its religious legitimacy, charitable endowments constituted the best forms of social solidarity among the individuals of the Islamic Society. These endowments provided cash and in rem capitals through which they supported various projects and works benefiting the humanity.

Experience of endowments doesn't only fruit at times of crises, but it also fruits at times of prosperity and bliss, as they are sufficient for various projects useful to the community and alleviate the burdens on the budgets of their countries. Consequently, such budgets are employed to support other prioritized projects . Interest in endowments, good deeds, spending money on needy people, and financing projects lacking material income, such as mosques, schools ... etc. emerged since Allah, Almighty called for that in His Noble Book, saying: (By no means shall you attain Al-Birr (Allah's Reward), unless you spend (in Allah's Cause) of that which you love; and whatever of good you spend, Allah knows it well) .(Surat Ale-Imran: Verse 92).

He also said: (O you who believe! Spend of the good things which you have (legally) earned, and of that which We have produced from the earth for you) (Surat Al-Baqarah: Verse 267).

He also said: (And whatever you spend in good, it will be repaid to you in full, and you shall not be wronged) (Surat Al-Baqarah: Verse 272)

He also said: (The believers are only those who, when Allah is mentioned, feel a fear in their hearts and when His Verses (this Quran) are recited unto them, they (i.e. the Verses) increase their Faith; and they put their trust in their Lord (Alone) (Surat Al-Anfal: Verses 2-4) Who perform As-Salat (Iqamat-as-Salat) and spend out of that We have provided them (Surat Al-Qasas: Verses 52-54) It is they who are the believers in truth. For them are grades of dignity with their Lord, and Forgiveness and a generous provision (Paradise) .

Waqf In Sunnah:

In Sunnah, It was narrated from Abu Hurairah that the Messenger of Allah said:

"When a man dies all his good deeds come to an end except three: Ongoing charity (Sadaqah Jariyah), beneficial knowledge and a righteous son who prays for him." Grade: Sahih (Darussalam)

Reference : Sunan an-Nasa'i 3651

In-book reference : Book 30, Hadith 41

English translation : Vol. 4, Book 30, Hadith 3681

In this context,Umar bin Khattab got some land in Khaibar and he went to the Prophet (ﷺ) to consult him about it saying, "O Allah's Messenger (ﷺ) I got some land in Khaibar better than which I have never had, what do you suggest that I do with it?" The Prophet (ﷺ) said, "If you like you can give the land as endowment and give its fruits in charity." So `Umar gave it in charity as an endowment on the condition that would not be sold nor given to anybody as a present and not to be inherited, but its yield would be given in charity to the poor people, to the Kith and kin, for freeing slaves, for Allah's Cause, to the travelers and guests; and that there would be no harm if the guardian of the endowment ate from it according to his need with good intention, and fed others without storing it for the future."

Reference : Sahih al-Bukhari 2737

In-book reference : Book 54, Hadith 24

USC-MSA web (English) reference : Vol. 3, Book 50, Hadith 895

(deprecated numbering scheme)

The purposes of waqf, however, are not confined to one's posterity, helping the poor and the needy and spending on the Qu'ran and mosques, but extend to cover schools, students, libraries, orphanages, attending to children, marriage, repatriation of strangers to their homeland, building hospitals, digging water wells, caring for animals, protection of environment and more other activities related to social development and solidarity.

The four eminent Islamic scholars have given different meaning of waqf or endowment as follows:

Al-Hanafi

The Hanafi Juristic School as: ((To keep a property as owned by Allah and give alms from its returns)) .

Waqf is to preserve and upkeep the original wealth that belonged to someone else and give the profit to the need.

By this we can learn that waqf is to preserve and upkeep wealth or something that can give benefit or profit, without being consummated by the original owner and give that benefit or profit to the needy.

Al-Maliki

The Maliki Juristic School as: ((To give the returns of something as long as it is existent and it has to be owned by the endower even if presupposedly)) .

Ownership of the profit from the origin of wealth which was given for endowment and gives it to whoever the endowment was meant for or the needy.

By this we understand that waqf is giving the right to consummate the profit of wealth that was given for endowment to whoever the endowment was meant for or the needy.

Al-Shafi`i

Waqf is to keep the wealth that can give benefit, and keep it remaining in the same form while the original owner cannot consume it.

We can learn that waqf is to keep a capital, which may be benefited from while its property shall not be disposed by the endower or any other person. Such capital shall be spent on good deeds to make the worshipper closer to Allah.

Hanbali

The Hanbali Juristic School as: ((To keep a capital and consecrate returns)). This last definition was quoted from the speech of the

Prophet (peace be upon him) to Umar Ibn Al Khattab (may Allah be pleased with him): ((If you wish you can keep it as an endowment to be used for charitable purposes)). This definition provided by Hanbalis is considered as one of the most abbreviated and clearest definitions. Therefore, through all these definitions, we can define endowment in general as the dedication of certain funds, productive capitals, or their returns or benefits for charitable private or public objectives, independently from personal disposal.

Waqf is keeping the original owner from consuming wealth that he had endowed, wealth which produce benefit should remain in the same form.

By this we can understand that waqf is wealth that was kept from the consummation of the original owner and give its benefit to the poor and needy, and that wealth must remain in the same condition without being consummate by the first owner.

From these four eminent scholars' views, we can learn that all scholars agreed that the waqf is to keep the origin wealth and use its profit for charity in order to help the poor and needy.

Types of Waqf:

Waqf is a permanent donation. Once a waqf is created, it can never be donated as a gift, inherited, or sold. Disbursement of its returns is done in accordance with the endower's wishes. Charity, on the other hand, is a broader concept; it encompasses alms, grant, inheritance, loan, waqf...

Family (Ahli) Waqf:

In this type of waqf, the usufruct goes to specific individuals or their posterity from among the relatives, descendants or otherwise. A waqif (dedicator) may request the usufruct to inure to a charitable agency in case the beneficiaries are extinct. Here, a waqf is initially a familial one, but finally it turns to a charitable one. The endower dedicates waqf to his family, children, relatives or others. Upon the death of the beneficiaries, this waqf may be transformed into a charitable one at the endower's request.

Charitable Waqf:

In this type of Waqf, the usufruct passes to one charitable body or more and spending here is made to bring a waqif nearer to Allah .The endowment is designated to help the poor, orphans, widows and for any other charitable causes.

Joint (Mushtarak) Waqf:

This waqf is a combination of both family and charitable awqaf.

Waqf components:

In a nutshell, a waqf functions as follows: a founder who has accumulated private wealth decides to endow his personal property for a specific, often, pious, purpose. The amount of the original capital, corpus, the purpose for which it is endowed and all the other conditions of management are clearly registered in a deed of endowment, submitted to the authorities. In this way the privately accumulated wealth of a pious Muslim becomes God's property.

The founder strictly stipulates how the annual revenue of the waqf should be spent. This revenue (usufruct) may be allocated completely for a pious purpose (waqf khayri), or to a group of beneficiaries. The offspring of the founder may also be the primary recipients of this annual revenue. Such waqfs are known as the family waqfs or waqf ahli. The management of the waqf is entrusted to a trustee, Nazir or Mutawalli, whose functions may be fulfilled by the founder himself during his lifetime. Thus, there are four major components of any waqf: the founder or endower , the beneficiaries, endowment (waqf) or the trustees and the endowed capital corpus itself.

Nazir or Mutawalli (administrator)

Nazir or Mutawalli are waqf trustees. Islamic law considers trustees strictly as managers to whom the waqf is entrusted. While these individuals were the ones who actually preserved the magnificent Islamic heritage through the centuries and enabled many waqfs to survive for centuries, it was also they who ended up being accused ruthlessly and held responsible for the demise of the system. It can be argued that all the major changes in the administration of the waqf system throughout history were undertaken in order to put these trustees under stricter control and end their opportunities for misuse and embezzlement. Sometimes accusations against them were justified, after all the trustees were only humans, but sometimes they were simply used as scapegoats and served the more sinister schemes of the state. The details of how the trustees fared as individuals crucial for the survival of the waqf system and as culprits, will be presented below.

Nazir or Mutawalli requirements:

The executor must have the following qualifications:

1. Be Muslim

2. Be mentally sane

3. Be mature in age.

4. Be just; a trustworthy individual who obeys the orders of Allah and is of good ethics and conduct.

5. Be wise; follow the endower's interest.

Nazir or Mutawalli 's duties:

It is the Nazir or Mutawalli 's responsibility to protect the waqf and maximize its investment:

1.Upkeep the waqf: undertake all maintenance and repair aimed at protecting and preserving the waqf from any damage.

2.Fulfill the endower's wishes.

3.Defend the waqf rights in any legal disputes.

4.Pay up waqf related debts

5.Spend the waqf revenues on the designated beneficiary and abide by the set date for disbursement, except in certain cases such as the need to pay up some waqf related debts.

Nazir or Mutawalli 's permissible and prohibited acts:

Nazir or Mutawalli has to right to perform any deeds beneficial to the waqf and to the endower within the conditions laid down by the endower.

Prohibited acts are those that might impact negatively on the waqf such as:

1.Lease the waqf for oneself or for one his children which is considered an act of nepotism.

2.Consider the waqf a guarantee for the executor's loan, in other words cover the payments of the executor's loan from the waqf revenues.

3.Pawn the waqf.

4.Lend the waqf to an individual or an institution other that the designated beneficiary.

5.Reside or have someone reside free of charge or for a minimal rent in the waqf estates.

III. Waqf over the years

Philanthropic foundations are known in the Islamic world as waqf or habs. Whereas the latter term is used primarily in North Africa, the former is known, with slight variations, in the rest of the Islamic world. The word waqf and its plural form awqaf are derived from the Arabic root verb waqafa, which means to cause a thing to stop and stand still. A second meaning is simply philanthropic foundations.

However, defined, this institution, whereby a privately owned property, corpus, is endowed for a charitable purpose in perpetuity and the revenue generated is spent for this purpose, stands out as one of the greatest achievements of Islamic civilization. All over the vast Islamic world, from the Atlantic to the Pacific, magnificent works of architecture as well as a wealth of services vitally important to the society have been financed and maintained for centuries through this system. It has even been argued that many waqfs had survived for considerably longer than half a millennium and some even for more than a millennium.

Despite these overwhelming achievements, the history of waqfs is a turbulent one. For centuries the fate of these institutions was closely linked to the fates of the states under which they functioned. Consequently, they experienced dramatic ups and downs: the period of establishment and growth was often followed by one of decline and neglect until with a new state emerging, renewal and prosperity once again prevailed.

Nowhere in this long history of fluctuations, however, did the waqfs experience the universal and deliberate destruction that was inflicted upon them during the nineteenth and twentieth centuries, a fact which pinpoints.

Ancient civilizations knew waqf long time ago and ancient records show that people in olden times, irrespective of their religious beliefs, knew some financial philanthropic practices, which come very near to the Islamic concept of waqf. Nevertheless, these practices differ from waqf in terms of purposes, motives and significance. There were some examples of charities and ahbas, which were dedicated to places of worship, the poor, the orphans, the needy and the disabled. For example, there were farms and properties whose proceeds were diverted to those charities. Consequently, something similar to waqf in form and content was set up, though different in its purposes and nomenclature.

With the emergence of Islam, as early as the epoch of the Prophet (PBUH) until the fall of the Ottoman Empire, Awqaf gained ground, showed a remarkable increase and played a prominent role in establishing a highly civilized Moslem state. Modern civilizations are believed to be complementary to past civilizations which accounts for the West's interest in trust (or waqf) and thereby creates modern formulas therefor.

As early as the emergence of Islam, waqf has been mainly connected with social development as revealed in the teachings of Islam which call for dedication as a means for getting nearer to Allah the Almighty. The mosques of Al Medina al Munawarra built up by the Prophet are considered the first waqf in

Islam. Likewise, the Prophet's companions (may Allah be pleased with them) followed the example of the Prophet so much so that Jaber (may Allah be pleased with him) says that none of the Prophet's well-off companions declined to establish a waqf.

Mosques won the lion's share in waqf in view of their vital role, though this process of dedication was not restricted to mosques (as we mentioned earlier) but extended to cover other areas of public utilities, such as water wells, farms, roads, etc...

This interest in Awqaf continued during the reign of the Fatimids, the Abbasids and the Ottomans until the fall of the Ottoman Empire. During the Ottoman era, waqf had administrative units tasked with caring for it and laws were set to organize, manage and define its types .

Islamic waqf played a prominent role in economic and cultural development and urbanization. Its effects, as we mentioned earlier, have extended largely to include various aspects of life. Such a distinctive historical role assisted in extending good services even during the periods of backwardness and imperialism .

The main domains for involvement in waqf can be put down as follows:

First: Attending to Mosques

The researcher divided the domains of waqf into: Constructing mosques and attending to them, Health services, Educational services and social services. It should be noticed that some domains are overlapped, for example, a waqf is made in favour of a university, with a hospital or mosques attached to it.

Second: Health Services

Health services took the lion's share Awqaf as shown in the establishment of hospitals which offered free treatment to poor patients, in addition to establishing waqf on medical education.

Third: Educational Services

Education and all that is related to it received due attention from Moslems as a result of their convictions that a society's stability can be secured only through the progress and evolution of education. Itis held as an ongoing human investment, which augments human resources development and improves skills and qualifications in the process of the social make-up. Stories about Moslems and their contributions are plentiful in history, all of which reflect that effective charitable role in developing the Islamic civilization.

Princess Fatima Bint Ismail was foremost among women who spent generously on promoting charitable work in the area of education and culture in Egypt. A considerable portion of the proceeds of her waqf was earmarked to support civil and military education in the seat of the Ottoman Caliphate. This woman takes great credit for establishing the Egyptian University (now the University of Cairo) at a time this project came nearly to a deadlock. Once this woman knew that the project was suffering from financial difficulties, she undertook to exert sincere efforts to execute that project. She allocated six acres out of her own best lands for the project to be erected on. Moreover, she allocated 661 acres in Daqahlia governorate out of 3357 acres allocated for charitable work to this project. The university's portion out of the proceeds of such lands amounted to 40% annually. The support extended by Princess Fatima expanded to cover sending talented students on scholarships inside and outside Egypt. In another initiative, Princess Fatima offered her own palace to the university on which the Agricultural Museum was built thereafter.

Fourth: Social Services

Moslems have always manifested a keen interest in playing an active role in social development through their contributions, which aimed at coping with the social needs which they sensed in their neighborhoods. Islam, as early as its emergence, developed this trend. In this respect, Nafi'e says:" Hafsa, may Allah be pleased with her, bought some jewels for twenty thousand and dedicated them to the women of al Ibn El Khattab. Because she paid no Zakat for such jewels, she used to use or lend them.

Similarly, Asma'a Bint Abi Bakr made her own house as a waqf so that it cannot be donated or bequeathed. Um El Mumineen Um Habiba Bint Abu Sufian dedicated a piece ofland to her servants and offspring so that this land cannot be sold, granted or bequeathed. During the Abbasid period, the mother of the caliph El Nasser established a waqf (Ribat, Ribat is a place for the poor or wayfarers) in Mekka El Mukarrama in 579 AH - 1183 AD.

Waqfs, so structured, stand out as one of the great achievements of Islamic civilisation. All over the vast Islamic world, from the Atlantic to the Pacific, magnificent works of architecture as well as services vitally important to the society such as education, health and many others have been organised, financed and maintained for centuries through this system.

Historians have established that the Islamic *waqf* law was borrowed by Europeans, particularly the English during the crusades, when they “visited” the Middle East and become acquainted with Islamic culture.

An excellent example is Merton College of Oxford University established in 1264. It is generally accepted that Merton College represents a threshold in the evolution of European universities. The Merton Foundation became a respected model in England and was emulated by the founding of Peterhouse, Cambridge University. Prof Gaudiosi has argued that the endowment deed of Merton College was in such conformity with the Islamic *waqf* law that it would have been approved in the Islamic world by any learned judge. In the

USA also, the top universities are either structured as *waqfs* (trusts) or they all have their own university endowments.

Returning back to the Islamic world, we note that according to the Hanafite law, when a privately owned property is endowed and is made the *corpus* of a *waqf*, it becomes Allah's property. This has made it rather difficult, but not entirely prevented, bankrupt and corrupt governments to confiscate *waqf* assets. Being relatively immune from confiscations, many *waqfs* with sound and sufficient endowments have survived for considerably longer than half a millennium and some even for more than a millennium.

Notwithstanding their longevity, the history of *waqfs* is a turbulent one. For centuries, the fate of this institution was closely linked to the fates of the states under which they functioned.

Failing states and desperate revenue seeking rulers had always a lust for the rich, *waqf*-controlled assets. This provocation could have been curbed somewhat had *waqfs* paid taxes to the state. But there were no uniform rules on this, while the Central Asian *waqfs* paid taxes depending upon their fiscal status before their establishment, neither the Malikite *waqfs* of Muslim Spain nor the Hanafite Ottoman cash *waqfs* of Bursa paid any taxes. Consequently, throughout Islamic history *waqf*-state relations have remained difficult. While on the one hand, the sultans established some of the greatest *waqfs*, on the other, the state often violated property rights of the *waqfs*, particularly if they were not legally sound.

Nowhere in this long history, however, did the *waqfs* experience the universal and deliberate destruction that was inflicted upon them during the 19th and 20th centuries, a fact which can be attributed directly to western imperialism or to the process of westernization. Usurpation of *waqf* properties started under western pressure and continued under the indigenous modernists even after Islamic countries gained independence. Consequently, in most of the Islamic world today, *waqfs* are dilapidated.

IV. Economics of Waqf

The institution of philanthropy—waqf, or Islamic endowment—is ideal for the creation and preservation of assets that can ensure flows of resources to provide education, health care, and other social goods. Waqf may also direct resources toward improving skills and developing human resources through technical assistance and capacity building. The social safety net, technical assistance, and capacity building may then be linked to financial assistance by helping to develop microenterprises. Thus, these Islamic financial institutions, by improving access to and the quality of education, health, and other social goods, can play a critical role in achieving the global goals of generating sufficient income earning opportunities and investing in people's development. These Islamic institutions can also serve to protect the poor and vulnerable against sudden risks of unemployment, hunger, illness, drought, and other calamities. These measures would greatly boost shared prosperity, improving the welfare of the least well-off. The Islamic approach to poverty alleviation is more inclusive than the conventional interventions based on microcredit. It provides for the basic conditions of sustainable and successful microfinance, blending wealth creation with empathy for the poorest of the poor. It favors models based on equity and cooperation, in contrast to mechanisms that tend to perpetuate debt. The discussion that follows briefly describes zakat and waqf as the key instruments of Islamic social finance that help reduce extreme poverty and boost shared prosperity. It presents brief case studies to highlight alternative models of intervention that utilize Islamic social finance.

Economists looking at the waqf system would be perplexed by the fact that a myriad of essential services such as health, education, municipal, etc., have historically been provided at no cost whatsoever to the government. Therefore, ceteris paribus, the waqf system can contribute significantly towards that ultimate goal of so many modern economists: massive reduction in government expenditure, which leads to a smaller budget deficit, which in turn lowers the need for government borrowing thus curbing the "crowding-out effect" and leads to a reduction in the rate of interest, consequently reining in a basic impediment to private investment and growth.

The waqf could fulfil these above-mentioned functions by voluntary donations made by the well to do. Thus, privately accumulated capital is voluntarily endowed to finance all sorts of social services to the society. At this point another extremely important function of the waqf becomes apparent: not only does it help reduce government expenditure and consequently the rate of interest and pave the way for growth, it also achieves another modern economic goal; a better distribution of income in the economy. For, this improvement in the distribution of income would be achieved essentially through voluntary donations. In this process taxation is definitively assigned a secondary role.

There are further implications: a lower tax burden means an enhancement in the consumers' and producers' surpluses and a diminution in the "dead-weight cost of the tax". Consequently, lower taxes would have a positive impact on aggregate production while at the same time reducing costs. Prices to the consumers would come down and pave the way for non-inflationary growth.

Moreover, the waqf definitely solves the problem of the under supply of public goods, so often observed in conventional economies. This point needs to be elaborated. In this context, we must first of all note that the services offered by the waqfs constitute public goods, the consumption of which is non-rivalrous and the provision thereof non-excludable.

As is well known, the standard economic theory envisages that since, as rational individuals, consumers of public goods tend to free ride, they fail to contribute to the costs of creating these goods. Consequently, where rational behavior prevails, public goods would be under produced in conventional economies.

As far as the Islamic world is concerned, there is much evidence to the contrary, i.e., to the ubiquitousness of the public goods supplied by the waqfs. Therefore, it seems more appropriate to talk about an excess supply of public goods rather than their scarcity. In an Islamic economy this excess supply, not scarcity, may emerge as the basic problem. It should be emphasized at this point that this observation is not confined to past history but is valid for all times. Indeed, there is no justification for the assumption that modern Muslims would be less interested in charity then their forefathers. Given the right conditions, modern Muslims have demonstrated that they are just as keen as their forefathers to establish waqfs. The latest evidence from Turkey concerning the dynamic expansion in the number of newly established waqfs confirms this.

All the social and economic contributions of the waqf system mentioned above, are based upon the crucial assumption that the waqfs are managed by prudent and efficient trustees. History, unfortunately, provides evidence that this was not often the case. Archives, indeed, are full of documents indicating the corruption of waqf officials. In short, there is a serious agency problem associated with the waqf system. This constitutes one of the greatest challenges to modern Islamic economists interested in revitalizing this system.

Traditional real estate *waqfs* functioned in a simple manner. They were either endowed in urban areas, where their endowment (*corpus*) would be in the form of residential buildings, shops, bath-houses or other rent yielding urban property, or in rural areas in which case their *corpus* would be in the form of cultivable land. In rural areas, the *waqf* land would be managed through sharecropping, *muzara'a*, with a certain share of the produce going to the land owning *waqf* and the rest to the cultivators. *Muzara'a* is the application of the classical *mudaraba* partnership in agriculture. In history, most arable lands in the Islamic world owned by *waqfs* were cultivated this way. In this arrangement, *waqf* provides the land and the produce can be shared between the *waqf* and the cultivator according to mutual agreement.

In order to fully understand the harm inflicted by the colonial and modernist policies directed against *waqfs*, the contribution of the *waqf* system to the economy must be well understood.

The *waqf* system has, throughout history provided a myriad of essential services such as health, education, municipal services, etc., to Islamic societies – to Muslims as well as non-Muslims. The system therefore contributes significantly towards that ultimate goal of so many modern economists i.e. with the *waqfs* providing the bulk of the financial needs of the service sector, there would be a substantial reduction in government expenditure. The reduction in government expenditure, on the other hand, would lead to a smaller budget deficit, which in turn, would lower the need for government borrowing.

This is precisely what the Chancellor of Germany, Angela Merkel, is trying to do in Europe today. She is forcing all member states to reduce government borrowing by not allowing the ECB to buy government bonds. In fact, she is simply telling them not to borrow! *Waqf* enters into the picture precisely here: it reduces the need for a government to borrow. Hence its modernity and relevance today is truly astounding!

Furthermore, a reduction in government borrowing would curb the crowding-out effect and lead to a reduction in the rate of interest, thereby curbing a basic impediment to private investment and growth.

Obviously, reducing the rate of interest, preferably to zero, would also be the ultimate goal of an Islamic government. To the extent that the *waqf* system contributes to the reduction/elimination of interest, it becomes an important tool for Islamic macro-economics. The *waqf* could fulfil these functions by voluntary donations made by the well-to-do. Thus, privately accumulated capital is voluntarily endowed to finance all sorts of social services to the society.

At this point another extremely important function of the *waqf* becomes apparent. Not only does it help reduce government expenditure and consequently, the rate of the prevailing interest and pave the way for growth while fulfilling an Islamic requirement, it also achieves another modern economic goal: a better distribution of income in the economy. Moreover, this improvement in the distribution of income would be achieved essentially through voluntary donations and the need for taxation is reduced. Thus, the relatively low tax burden of an Islamic economy must be considered within a broader context that includes the *waqf* system. Indeed, the tax burden in an Islamic economy can be low because the bulk of the essential services should be provided by the *waqfs*. Tax revenues are earmarked primarily for defence. This is not just theory. Ottoman budget studies have confirmed that indeed this was the case

There are further implications as well: lower taxes would have a positive impact on aggregate production while at the same time reduce costs. Prices would come down and pave the way for non-inflationary growth.

Thus those Islamic economists who argue for increasing taxation despite the Qur`anic injunctions, are missing the point. The Qur`an, mentioning just a small number of modest taxes, is actually giving us a message that the government should be small – a very modern concept! Thus, instead of trying to impose taxes that are not in the Qur`an, they should focus on reforming the *waqf* system because a well-functioning *waqf* system would allow the economy to function with minimum taxation. The Ottoman experience of channeling all tax revenues for defense and financing all essential services through *waqfs* confirms that this is possible.

One of the most important of these services is education. Education serves both growth and equity. Throughout history it was the *waqf* system which provided education and health in Islamic countries. These two are the most important components of human capital and this is the secret of the successes of countries such as Japan, Taiwan and South Korea, all without natural resources.

There is no doubt that centralization and the damage inflicted upon the *waqf* system has been detrimental to the development of these services in the Islamic world. It is clear that the state provided education and health services have not been a match for the *waqf* provided one. At the very least, the *waqf* system is needed to supplement the state provided education and health sectors.

The positive impact of the *waqfs* on employment should also be acknowledged. Partly as a consequence, Western countries have now reversed their traditional hostilities to trusts/foundations. The French government, which used to be the most anti-*waqf* government throughout history, now subsidizes 60% of the expenditure of French foundations. The result, all over the west, was a significant increase in employment. The non-profit sector accounted for an average of 13% of the net jobs added between 1980-1990 in France, Germany and the United States. In the U.S., the non-profit sector accounts for 6.9% of total employment. It has been reported that currently a massive "revolution" is taking place in the US philanthropy. Clearly, in addition to all the advantages mentioned above, the revival of the system would contribute to the solution to the problem of employment in the Islamic world as well.

Waqfs may also play a significant role in the democratization of Islamic countries. This is because *waqfs* constituted for centuries civil society institutions *par excellence* for the Islamic world. Indeed, established with private capital, which was often pooled, they were decentralized, autonomous decision making units involved in local problems. It is quite possible that the incapacitating policies imposed on the *waqf* system for the last 200 years have deprived the Islamic world of its most potent democratic force.

Thus, lack of democracy is not, as some believe, an outcome of Islam as a religion, but a consequence of the last two centuries of institutional and economic history.

V. Maximizing Social Impact Through Waqf Solutions

Islamic endowment is a multi-purpose organization. It has been initiated and it practices its activities in accordance with legal systems derived from the provisions of Islamic Shariah. It is operated within the scope of ever-changing organizational and administrative frameworks which are affected by modern systems. This great organization has to remain a pioneering institution in this field by rejecting any calls for stagnancy under the pretext of originality. The endowment organization should avoid any attempts to paralyze its movement through outdated organizational and administrative frameworks and the adoption thereof without taking the orientation towards the necessities of development. Such development should be commensurate with life contemporary updates without compromising legitimate basics.

this context, contemporary organizational and administrative development produces many frameworks and applications which target at promoting the performance level of the public and private organizations.

The above-mentioned ideas and applications include governance which is a global phenomenon which has been implemented in governmental authorities, civil society and non-governmental organizations. At the outset, its implementation has been limited to financial and economic companies and institutions.

Although the idea of governance is still new and its application is limited outside the realms of financial and economic institutions, the stakeholders in charge of the endowment organization are looking forward to making use of it and introducing applied models which are more consistent with the nature of endowment and the peculiar features of the endowment organization.

Governance is one of the principal constituents of good management. It guarantees transparency, disclosure, accountability, limitation of liability, and making sure that the endowment administration adheres to legitimate provisions, applicable laws and systems, codes of conduct, Islamic morals, and all endowment-related regulations. Such guarantees shall contribute to maintaining the endowment, its assets, properties and beneficiaries' rights. They generate confidence in endowment and create a positive image on it in the whole society. Besides, they contribute to protecting the endowment from the risks resulting from mismanagement.

The significance of endowment governance is highlighted by addressing the facets of defects in managing endowment, generating confidence on the level of both the endowers and the beneficiaries, extending the bridges of trust among them and increasing the value of the endowed capitals.

Governance is a multi-tiered administrative system. Its roles are integrated in order to reach good management by realizing the specific objectives of the system as well as all its elements. The most important tools of governance include laws, systems, policies, codified procedures which regulate work in the field of endowment, balanced organizational structure commensurate with the volume and purposes of endowment, financial and accounting reports which enable the endowment stakeholders to follow up the performance of the management bodies, disbursement of its revenues and the identification of the levels of the management efficiencies. For these tools to be effective, the following requirements should be fulfilled:

- A solid accounting infrastructure
- Allowing the endower, heirs, some designated beneficiaries and other external stakeholders to participate in the committees and councils co-managing the endowment
- An effective system of reporting, accountability, internal control and external audit

- Effective judicial control
- An integrated document including the ethical standards adopted by the endower .

On the other hand, Waqf foundations need a steady stream of revenue in order to fund their operations. They cannot achieve financial sustainability by relying entirely on donations. Many are finding it necessary to expand their revenue base to include steadier forms of income from assets in their custody and from other commercial activities and investments. Thus, their social work is getting more closely entwined with business interests.

Toward the Optimal Mobilization of *Waqf* Resources

waqf could meet the resource gap to eradicate extreme poverty, the actual returns are dismal.

Studies show widespread usurpation of *waqf* assets by both State and non-State actors, as well as leasing of *waqf* assets at rates that are grossly below market.

With respect to mobilization of *waqf* resources, data indicate a near-freeze in the creation of new social *waqf*, though religious *waqf* continue to be created. Places of worship (*masjids)* and seminaries (*madrasas*) have increased in numbers, especially where new Muslim communities have emerged. There has been some rejuvenation of social *waqf* in the form of cash *waqf* in Indonesia, Malaysia, and Singapore. Some development of *waqf* assets and their prudent investment to generate returns has also occurred in these countries, as well as in Sudan, which is also known for its successful family *waqf*.

Importance of waqf in Supporting Voluntary Works

Any researcher of Islamic history can note that it is easy for any rich persons performing good deeds in the various Islamic countries to give alms and volunteer through constructing mosques and their extensions such as kuttabs (places of Quran memorization) and housing affiliated to them, and supporting them with workers, muezzins, Imams, and laborers assuming works of cleaning and serving water for performers of prayers and students. It is also easy for them to construct schools and their extensions such as accommodation of students, orphans, and workers as well as their kitchens dedicated for preparing various meals for students, equip such schools with required furniture and lighting, and hire teachers, teaching assistants, and workers. They can also volunteer through providing water endowments on roads … etc. The problem facing such volunteers is their obligation to provide the continuous financial support for such charitable religious and educational facilities and their volunteering laborers, so that they can perform their religious, human, and moral duties. Therefore, such volunteers, specially rich persons, focused from the very beginning of constructing such facilities on the issue of financial support. They searched for sustainable finance sources to spend on them, their laborers and volunteers. So, they did not find any source better than endowments as a sustainable solution for their finance problems. Therefore, they provide as endowments the best of their capitals, orchards, farms, and real estate which returns suffice such projects, including their laborers and volunteers, aiming at providing the sustainability of returns for such facilities to serve humankind and provide a recurring charity until the Day of Resurrection.

Experiences of previous nations highlight the importance of endowments in supporting volunteers in charge of places of worship and the persons assigned to serve their visitors for worship and Hajj.

Waqfs support of small business

Waqf organizations are viewed as centers of community service and assistance. Waqfs can use the small business model to serve their objectives.

Evidence from many countries points to the vital role that partnerships between waqfs and small businesses play in community development.

Waqfs can be a catalyst for growth of the small- and medium-sized enterprises (SMEs). Waqfs can raise capital and channel funds into the hands of competent management who have business propositions that have the best prospects of succeeding.

Waqfs' support is not a matter of just providing finance or giving loans to existing small businesses. They build new capabilities and sustainable ventures. Waqf organizations can be the "business angels" entering into partnerships with start-up entrepreneurs as well as early-stage and developing businesses. Such partnerships can be of enormous benefit to the project, the waqf organization and the entrepreneur.

Waqfs' Financial Support

Waqfs' financial support can be in any one of the three main Shari'ah compliant modes: participatory, concessionary and project financing. Within these modes are various contractual forms that conform fully to the principle of profit and loss sharing.

Participatory SME financing is the most flexible and most common as it adheres to the Islamic principles of sharing of risks and profits. This is a process wherein a waqf instead of lending money to an enterprise actually gets involved as a partner or shareholder in the business. The more commonly used participatory modes are musharaka (equity participation) and mudaraba (trust financing). From an SME stance, participatory funding is a good alternative to higher-cost borrowing.

Musharaka participation by waqf facilitates the transfer of a pre-determined share of the risk

in return for a share in the profit. In Mudarabah , waqf as the finance provider (rabul mal) promotes business development by extending financing to capable but cash-strapped entrepreneurs, waqfs, therefore, carry the financial risk and share profits at a pre-agreed percentage.

Concessionary financing is money advanced mainly in the form of qard hasan (benevolent loan) where only the principal is to be repaid. It can also be loans at below-market rates—usually at a small service charge to cover administrative costs. The cash waqf is the main source for concessionary SME financing. Concessionary lending can only be considered in low-risk operations and with adequate safeguards to ensure repayment.

Project financing modes are usually non-profit-sharing, as they are based on cost plus a pre-determined mark-up. The financing contracts used include baimuajjal (instalment sales), baisalam (forward sale contracts), ijara (lease financing), ijarawaiqtina (hire-purchase), istisna'a (construction/manufacturing finance) and murabaha (procurement financing).

The choice of the mode of financing and the type of contract depends on the nature and needs of the project, the risk profile and expected returns, and on the waqf organization's own investment policy and guidelines.

Waqf's Non-financial Support

Waqf can also provide a whole gamut of non-financial support for the smaller enterprise. The most common in-kind contribution is land. The provision of land for a project serves waqf developmental objectives of waqf properties and ensures permanent connection of the project to the waqf organization. In such arrangements, the appraised current market value of the land is used to determine the waqf's share in the project.

Other in-kind support includes services such as consultancy and training, guidance and monitoring and insurance.

Waqf organizations can also serve as business incubators for new ventures, nurturing and helping them to survive and prosper. Waqf can provide advice and guidance and help in areas of strategic planning, which can be particularly helpful during the early stages of business development.

Role of Waqf in Establishing Fair and Affordable Prices

The integration of waqf with the market has yielded positive results in terms of providing microfinance, education, and health care at affordable prices to the poor and excluded. A case in point is provision of health care by the Waqaf al-Noor, an innovative corporate waqf that was structured by the Johor Corporation of Malaysia. Waqf may also directly contribute to the success of Islamic microfinance experiments to improve the economic lot of the poor.

Islamic economists have often sought to make microfinance more affordable by suggesting an integration of zakat and/or waqf with microfinance. A cash waqf with returns dedicated to fully or partly absorb the cost of financial and nonfinancial services may be able to ensure that loans are offered at zero or low cost, making them interest-free as well as affordable for the poorest of the poor.

Nowhere is this phenomenon better documented than in Bangladesh, which is often referred to as the "university of microfinance." Fa'el Khair Waqf offers a real-life example of this exciting solution to poverty and destitution .

Policy Recommendations to Better Mobilize *Waqf* Resources

1. *Waqf,* in general, have fallen behind common trusts and other forms that are organizing charitable and nonprofit activities in response to evolving social needs. Creation and management of *waqf* is a relatively more complex and demanding process and involves

additional financial and nonfinancial costs. Incentivizing *waqf* in a manner similar to secular trusts and other forms of nonprofit organizations, such as through tax rebates on contributions for the donor/endower, would make the system both efficient and fair.

2. The legal framework should make it possible for all segments of the society to establish *waqf*. Currently, some laws restrict making a *waqf* only to Muslim individuals. Laws should permit both non-Muslims and institutions to establish *waqf* as long as the purpose of *waqf* is religious or charitable.

3. The legal framework should not restrict the definition of the endowed asset to immovable tangible assets, such as real estate, but should also explicitly recognize movable, financial, and intangible assets, such as cash, equities, bonds and financial securities, transportation

vehicles, rights on land and buildings, leasing rights, and intellectual property rights.

Toward Better Management of *Waqf* Resources

Prudent *waqf* management requires preservation and development of the *waqf* assets, investment and generation of returns, and ensuring that the returns/benefits flow to the beneficiaries as intended by the *waqif*.

1. Preservation of *waqf* is the most important concern in *waqf* management. The legal framework must clearly articulate the permanent nature of *waqf* arising from the principle of “Once a *waqf*, always a *waqf*.” In case old laws fail to ensure protection, they must be replaced with new provisions that enable recovery of lost *waqf* assets. A good example is the Sudanese law that empowers the Diwan to recover all the endowed money

that is possessed by other individuals, institutions, companies, or governmental authorities or to receive just and equitable compensation from them.

2. *Waqf* is an institution originally and always meant to be in the voluntary sector, with management of *waqf* entrusted to private parties. However, the State has often sought to play a role in the ownership and management of *waqf* assets, at times governed by motives to expropriate, and at other times, by the need to curb the corrupt practices of private trustee-managers. There is no clear answer to the question of whether ownership and management of *waqf* assets should be in private hands or with the State. There seems to be some positive evidence that the State can play the role of an efficient manager of *waqf* assets.

Contrary to general belief, State control may not necessarily hamper creativity and innovation in *waqf* development.

Positive examples include corporate *waqf* as well as cash *waqf* in Malaysia, and large-scale development of existing *waqf* assets in the public-private mode in Malaysia, Singapore, and Sudan.

3. Where *waqf* management is in private hands, the State agency as regulator should clearly stipulate elaborate and clear eligibility criteria for a *mutawalli* or *nazir,* or trustee-manager, not only covering aspects of integrity and trustworthiness but also professional competence.

If the individual or institution so nominated meets the criteria, the regulator must respect the expressed intention of the *waqif* or endower. Laws must clearly articulate the responsibility of *waqf* management to emphasize not only preservation and protection of *waqf* assets, but also their development.

The responsibility should also include transparent and honest reporting of financial assets and transactions.

Laws must clearly stipulate the method of determining remuneration of managers, sufficiently incentivizing sound and professional management of *waqf* assets.

The laws in Indonesia and Mauritius provide good examples related to these matters. The law stipulates that the remuneration to which a *mutawalli* is entitled shall not exceed one-tenth of the income of the *waqf*.

4. There is every reason for the State to take punitive action against *mutawallis* who are negligent or lack integrity and transparency. The measures must act as effective deterrents against further acts of carelessness, neglect, and misappropriation. At the same time, the State should not be allowed to wield absolute power to engage in irrational or whimsical action against the *mutawalli*. Instances of unfair and unlawful action by the State are numerous, as are cases of corrupt *mutawallis*. There is need for effective checks and balances in the law against wrongful acts by both the State and private *mutawallis*. Power has a tendency to corrupt, and the possibility of such action can significantly increase the nonfinancial cost of creating new *waqf*. Endowers are likely to seek alternative forms of organizing their charitable activities if there is a

possibility of undue State interference in the management of the endowed assets or outright usurpation of the endowed assets by the State.

5. It is compulsory to invest *waqf* assets, whether they are real estate or movable assets like cash. Investment can generate returns, which may then be applied to the purpose for which the *waqf* has been created. The assets purchased using the *waqf* investment returns do not form part of the *waqf,* and therefore may be resold, unlike the original assets that have been given as *waqf.* Further, the conditions given by the endower or *waqif* with regard to the investment of the *waqf* or conditions that the returns from investment are to be spent on specific areas are also binding. It would be rational to try to minimize risks through diversification or avoidance of high-risk investment activities. Risk minimization,

however, may not be sought if the purpose of the *waqf* itself is to engage in specific risky ventures.

Policy Recommendations to Integrate Waqf with Microfinance

Microfinance entails high administrative charges, monitoring costs, and of course, high portfolio risk. Thus it is invariably costlier than the traditional sources of finance. At the same time, both the microfinance institution and its clients may find this an attractive option if they believe that the expected return on the microenterprise is higher than the cost of debt. Such expectations may indeed materialize for the successful projects during "good times." However, the same may not be true for all projects at all times. Debt-related liability can compound and accentuate the financial problems of a project experiencing bad times and hasten its failure. The pace, frequency, and intensity of such failure is directly related to the levels of cost of debt. In contrast to debt, profit- and risk-sharing mechanisms provide a clear alignment between the profitability of the project and cost of capital. The latter rises and falls in line with the realized profits of the venture. Islamic MFIs, as compared to conventional MFIs, are more inclined to use profit- and risk sharing modes. Even when they use financing methods that create debt such as *murabahah*, the amount of debt once created cannot be increased through restructuring if the client fails to repay the debt on time. Further, given the Islamic emphasis on avoidance of debt, an Islamic MFI should refrain from seeking to entrap a client in ever-rising levels of debt.

For-profit *Shari'ah*-compliant methods of financing offer no built-in protection against exploitation and abuse through overpricing. Enhancing the financial literacy of poor clients is perhaps the only effective bulwark against such exploitation. The following examples clearly highlight the possibility of exploitation, and therefore the need for financial literacy:

a. Returns on micro-*murabahah* and micro-*ijarah* financing are deemed *shari'ah* compliant, while interest rates are not. However, both can be, and often are, high to the point of exploitation.

b. In case of participatory modes of finance such as *murabah, musharakah,* and *mudharaa,* the sharing ratio could be unfairly biased against the poor beneficiary because of their low bargaining power. Similarly, in case of feebased financing through *wakalah* and *haawalah*, the agent-microfinance institution may charge an exorbitant fee for the same reasons.

c. The permissibility of *salam* (sale of nonexistent produce) is linked to the economic benefits it confers on poor farmers who need financing before they can cultivate their crops or produce their agricultural goods. However, *salam* can involve exploitation when the advance price paid to the poor farmer is artificially pegged at low levels due to his or her weak bargaining power.

An Islamic economy promotes free pricing and allows intervention by the regulator only when natural forces of demand and supply are manipulated to result in an artificial price. By implication, price ceilings or administered prices are frowned upon in a market where there is free and fair play of competitive forces in the determination of prices. However, in the case of financing methods where the regulator is in a position to determine a fair estimate of the costs for the MFI, it may seek to regulate the profit margin so that prices charged by MFIs ensure full cost recovery and a fair amount of returns in the interest of sustainability. At times, identifying an appropriate organizational structure may offer a bulwark against possible exploitation. For example, in the case of *salam*, a farmer's cooperative may replace the vendor and thus prevent exploitation of individual farmers by the latter.

References:

Ahmed, H. (2007). Waqf-based microfinance: Realizing the social role of Islamic finance. *World Bank*.

Al Humaidan, Iman Mohamed. (2007). Woman and Waqf. Kuwait: Awqaf Public Foundation, Department of Studies and External Relations, 1st. edition, 1428AH.

Al Omar, F. A. (2013). *Contribution of Waqf to Non-Governmental Work and Social Development*. Kuwait Kuwait Awqaf Public Foundation.

AWQAF Journal, Editorial, Governance: Pathway of the Endowment Organizations towards Rationalized Management, AWQAF

Journal,16th Year, No.31, Safar 1438 / Nov. 2016

Banday, B. (2009). *Administration of wakfs Law and practice in Kashmir.* (Doctor of Philosophy in Law), University of Kashmir.

Bank;, W., & Group, I. D. B. (2017). *Global Report on Islamic Finance : Islamic Finance - A Catalyst for Shared Prosperity?. Washington, DC: World Bank. © Islamic Development Bank Group.* https://openknowledge.worldbank.org/handle/10986/25738 *License: CC BY 3.0 IGO.".* Retrieved from

Chowdhury, M. S. R., bin Ghazali, M. F., & Ibrahim, M. F. (2011). Economics of Cash WAQF management in Malaysia: A proposed Cash WAQF model for practitioners and future researchers. *African Journal of Business Management, 5*(30), 12155.

Cizakca, M. (1997). Towards a comparative economic history of the waqf system. *Al-Shajarah, 6*, 63-102.

Çizakça, Murat. (2000). A history of philanthropic foundations: The Islamic world from the seventh century to the present. Istanbul: Boğaziçi University Press .

Çizakça, Murat. "A Critical Assessment of the *Waqf* Law Being Prepared by IDB/IRTI and Kuwait Foundation", in Mehmet Kurtoğlu (ed.), *Dünya Vakıflar Konferansı* (World *Waqfs* Conference), (Ankara: VGM Yayınları No. 113, 2014). Also available in www.academia.edu.

Çizakça, Murat. *Islamic Capitalism and Finance* (Cheltenham: E. Elgar, 2011).

Dallal, A. (2004). The Islamic Institution of

Waqf, "The Islamic Institution of Waqf." Islam and Social Policy. Ed. Steve Heyneman. Nashville: Vanderbilt University Press, 13-43

Duasa, J., & Thaker, M. A. B. M. T. (2016). A Cash Waqf Investment Model: An Alternative Model for Financing Micro-enterprises in Malaysia *Journal of Islamic Monetary Economics and Finance, 1*(2), 161-188.

Harasani, H. (2015). *Toward the Reform of Private Waqfs: A Comparative Study of Islamic Waqfs and English Trusts*: Brill.

Heyneman, S. P. (2004). *Islam and social policy*: Vanderbilt University Press.

Ibrahim, H., Amir, A., & Masron, T. A. (2013). Cash Waqf: An Innovative Instrument for Economic Development. *International Review of Social Sciences and Humanities, 6*(1), 1-7.

Kahf, M. (1999a). Financing the Development of" Awqaf" Property. *American Journal of Islamic Social Sciences, 16*(4), 39.

Kahf, M. (1999b). *Towards the revival of awqaf: A few fiqhi issues to reconsider.* Paper presented at the Harvard forum on Islamic finance and Economics.

Kahf, M. (2003). *The role of waqf in improving the ummah welfare.* Paper presented at the International Seminar on Waqf as a Private Legal Body, organised by the Islamic University of North Sumatra, Medan, Indonesia.

Mohsin, I. A. (2015). Waqf and Islamic banking and finance: The missing link. *Global Islamic Finance Report (GIFR) 2015, pp 113-121.*

Mohsin, I. A. (2015). Waqf and Islamic banking and finance: The missing link. Global Islamic Finance Report (GIFR) 2015, pp 113-121.

Mohsin, M. I. A. (2016). The Role of Waqf in Modern Economic Development *Financing the Development of Old Waqf Properties* (pp. 21-35): Springer.

Mohsin, M. I. A. (2016). The Role of Waqf in Modern Economic Development Financing the Development of Old Waqf Properties (pp. 21-35): Springer.

Mohsin, M. I. A., Dafterdar, H., Cizakca, M., Alhabshi, S. O., Razak, S. H. A., Sadr, S. K., . . . Obaidullah, M. (2016a). Legal Framework of the Institution of Waqf *Financing the Development of Old Waqf Properties: Classical Principles and Innovative Practices around the*

World (pp. 1-12). New York: Palgrave Macmillan US.

Mohsin, M. I. A., Dafterdar, H., Cizakca, M., Alhabshi, S. O., Razak, S. H. A., Sadr, S. K., . . . Obaidullah, M. (2016b). The Role of Waqf in Modern Economic Development *Financing the Development of Old Waqf Properties: Classical Principles and Innovative Practices around the World* (pp. 21-35). New York: Palgrave Macmillan US.

Mohsin, M. I. A., Dafterdar, H., Cizakca, M., Alhabshi, S. O., Razak, S. H. A., Sadr, S. K., . . . Obaidullah, M. (2016a). Legal Framework of the Institution of Waqf Financing the Development of Old Waqf Properties: Classical Principles and Innovative Practices around the World (pp. 1-12). New York: Palgrave Macmillan US.

Mohsin, M. I. A., Dafterdar, H., Cizakca, M., Alhabshi, S. O., Razak, S. H. A., Sadr, S. K., . . . Obaidullah, M. (2016b). The Role of Waqf in Modern Economic Development Financing the Development of Old Waqf Properties: Classical Principles and Innovative Practices around the World (pp. 21-35). New York: Palgrave Macmillan US.

Noordin, N. H., Haron, S. N., & Kassim, S. (2017). Developing a comprehensive performance measurement system for Waqf institutions. *International Journal of Social Economics, 44*(7).

Othman Ahmed Othman, Financial Estate of Endowment, AWQAF Journal, 16th Year, No.30, Rajab 1437 / May 2016.

Saiti, B. (2016). Islamic Capitalism and Finance: Origins, Evolution and the Future

International Journal of Economics, Management and Accounting, 24(1), 125-128.

Salarzehi, H., Armesh, H., & Nikbin, D. (2010). Waqf as a social entrepreneurship model in Islam. *International Journal of Business and Management, 5*(7), 179.

Sanusi, S., & Shafiai, M. H. M. (2015). The management of cash waqf: toward socio-economic development of Muslims in Malaysia. *Jurnal Pengurusan, 43*, 3-12.

Stibbard, P., QC, D. R., & Bromley, B. (2012). Understanding the waqf in the world of the trust. *Trusts & Trustees, 18*(8), 785.

Tan Sri Muhammad Ali Hashim,Corporate Waqf – a proposal for corporate reform.at: https://infocus.wief.org/corporate-waqf-proposal-corporate-reform-bridge-divides-uphold-economic-justice/

Taha Hussein Awad Hudail,Charitable Endowments and their Role in Supporting Voluntary Work Study of a Source and Method of Financing Voluntary Services in Hajj and Umrah, AWQAF Journal, 16th Year, No.30, Rajab 1437 / May 2016.

Yalawae, A., Tahir, I. M., UDM, U. D. I. M., & Campus, K. (2003). The Role of Islamic Institution in Achieving Equality and Human Development: Waqf or Endowment. Universiti Darul Iman Malaysia (UDM).

Yasser Abdulkareem Al Horany ,Governance of the Endowment of Productive Resources, AWQAF Journal, 16th Year, No.30, Rajab 1437 / May 2016.

www.ingramcontent.com/pod-product-compliance
Lightning Source LLC
Chambersburg PA
CBHW050531240926
51846CB00003B/770
* 9 7 8 2 8 0 8 5 9 5 3 3 9 *